The
Buffalo

Published by Raintree Steck-Vaughn Publishers, an imprint of Steck-Vaughn Company.

Acknowledgments
Project Editor: Pam Wells
Design Manager: Joyce Spicer
Editor: Sabrina Crewe
Designers: Ian Winton and Steve Prosser
Consultant: Michael Chinery
Illustrator: Robert Morton
Electronic Cover Production: Alan Klemp
Additional Electronic Production: Scott Melcer
Photography credits on page 32

Planned and produced by The Creative Publishing Company

Library of Congress Cataloging-in-Publication Data
    Crewe, Sabrina
    The buffalo / Sabrina Crewe ; [illustrator, Robert Morton].
        p.   cm. — (Life cycles)
    Includes index.
    Summary: Provides an introduction to the life cycle, physical characteristics, behavior, and habitat of a plains bison.
    ISBN 0-8172-4377-1 (hardcover). — ISBN 0-8172-6238-5 (pbk.)
    1. American bison — Juvenile literature. 2. American bison — Life cycles — Juvenile literature. [1. Bison.] I. Morton, Robert, ill. II. Title. III. Series: Crewe, Sabrina. Life cycles.
QL737.U53C74 1998
599.64'3 — dc21   96-40494
                                    CIP   AC

 2 3 4 5 6 7 8 9 0 LB 01 00 99 98
Printed and bound in the United States of America.

Words explained in the glossary appear in **bold** the first time they are used in the text.

The
Buffalo

Sabrina Crewe

RSVP ®

RAINTREE
STECK-VAUGHN
P U B L I S H E R S
The Steck-Vaughn Company

Austin, Texas

The buffalo calf has just been born.

It is spring. The buffalo **cow** has a new calf. Half an hour after it is born, the calf can stand on its wobbly legs. Its mother licks it clean.

The calf feeds on its mother's milk.

The calf is one week old. Its legs have grown stronger. The buffalo cow **nurses** the calf. At first, the calf gets all the food it needs from its mother's milk.

The calf lives in a herd.

The calf and its mother live in a group with other buffalo. Their group is called a herd. Other cows and their calves live with the herd. So do the young adult buffalo. The older **bulls** stay in their own herd for part of the year.

The calf is playing with its mother.

Living in a herd helps keep the calves safe. But they are still at risk from **predators** when they are very young. The new calves stay close to their mothers all the time.

The calf is grazing.

As the calf grows older, it learns to **graze** like the older buffalo. The calf still nurses, but now it can eat grass and drink water, too.

The calves have little horns.

When the calves are six or seven weeks old,
they start to grow horns. At first their horns
are just small bumps. The calves play with
each other, running around the herd and
butting their heads together.

The herd is traveling.

The herd is always moving slowly, looking for food. The oldest cow leads the herd as it travels. In summer, the buffalo find many plants growing near the river.

The calf is growing a hump.

The calf is a few months old. It has grown much bigger, and its horns are growing, too. The hump on its neck is starting to show. The calf's fur is changing color. Soon its light-colored coat will be dark brown all over.

The calf grows thick fur for winter.

By the time winter comes, the calf has grown a thick, dark coat of fur. Buffalo grow extra fur in winter to keep out the cold. When the snow is deep, the buffalo use their strong heads to plow through the snow and find food.

The buffalo find food under the snow.

The herd keeps traveling to look for food. They are grazing near a **hot spring**. The snow around the hot spring is less thick, and the buffalo have found some grass to eat.

The bulls run and jump.

In spring the young bulls are full of energy. When the buffalo are one year old, they start to look after themselves. Buffalo become **mature** when they are two or three years old. The cows stay with their herd, but the bulls leave to join the other bulls.

The buffalo is cooling off.

By summer, buffalo lose most of their thick winter fur. They still need to find ways to keep cool. The middle of the day gets very hot. The buffalo cools off by swimming in the cold river water.

The buffalo rolls in the dust.

Buffalo get very itchy in summer. Their fur is home to many bugs that feed on their skin and blood. The buffalo is rolling and rubbing its body on the ground. This stops the itching from bug bites. Rolling also covers the buffalo in dirt that helps keep bugs away.

The cowbirds ride on the buffalo's back.

Birds that sit on the buffalo's back are very useful. The cowbirds eat the bugs that live in the buffalo's fur.

The herd is stampeding.

When buffalo get scared by something, they start to run. If one buffalo runs, the rest of its herd will follow. Other herds they pass will join the **stampede**.

From a distance, hundreds of running buffalo sound like thunder. Buffalo herds will sometimes stampede for many miles.

The bulls charge at each other.

In the middle of summer, many buffalo herds come together. The adult bulls join the herds of cows and calves. The bulls charge and fight with their heads and horns. After a while, one bull gives up. The other one has shown that he is the strongest.

The bull finds a mate.

The bulls that win fights are the ones that will mate with the cows. At the end of summer, the bulls leave the cows again. Nine months after the bull and cow have mated, a new calf will be born.

Buffalo need open spaces.

For thousands of years, buffalo herds traveled through the open land of North America. Then people decided they should all be killed. Millions of buffalo died, and there were very few left. Now buffalo are protected by people. They live in parks where the land is kept wild for them and other animals.

Legends of the Buffalo

In the days when millions of buffalo lived in North America, they shared the land with Native Americans. Buffalo were very important to Native Americans. Native Americans hunted buffalo for food. They used buffalo skin and fur to keep warm. They used the bones and horns for tools and weapons.

Native Americans believed buffalo were **sacred**.
Many tribes still tell **legends** about the buffalo.
One legend says that a buffalo taught a sacred
dance to some Native Americans. Before and
after a buffalo hunt, the Native Americans
would perform the dance. This would bring the
spirits of the buffalo back to life.

Parts of a Buffalo

Buffalo belong to a group of **mammals** called **bovids**. Like most mammals, bovids are covered in fur and feed their young with milk. All bovids have horns on their heads and hooves on their feet. Bovids feed on grass and other plants that grow where they live.

Fur
Thick for warmth
and protection

Hooves
Hard covering
protects feet

Hump
Made of bone and muscle
Supports large head

Horns
Used to protect and attack

Head
Large and broad
for pushing snow
to uncover grass

Eyes
Small with weak sight

Nose
Good sense of smell

Teeth
Sharp front teeth
for cutting plants
Flat back teeth for
grinding

Other Bovids

The buffalo in this book has another name. Some people call it the plains bison. There are two other types of bison: the wood bison in Canada and the wisent in Europe. There are also other kinds of buffalo. You can see them here, with some other bovids.

Yak

Mountain goat

Domestic cow

Bighorn sheep

Cape buffalo

Water buffalo

Wisent

Wood bison

29

Where the American Buffalo Lives

Alaska
(U.S.)

CANADA

UNITED
STATES

Areas where
the American
buffalo lives

MEXICO

30

Glossary

Bovid A kind of mammal with horns and hooves that eats only plants

Bull The adult male of certain kinds of animals, including buffalo

Cow The adult female of certain kinds of animals, including buffalo

Graze To feed on growing grass

Hot spring A place where warm or hot water comes out of the ground

Legend A very old story that has special meaning for one group of people

Mammal A kind of animal that usually has fur and feeds its young with milk

Mature Fully developed

Nurse To feed young animals with mother's milk

Predator An animal that hunts and kills other animals for food

Sacred Something that is special or has to do with people's faith

Stampede A large group of frightened animals running away

Index

Photography credits